# *Architecture of Scotland*

The Author

GEORGE HAY, A.R.I.B.A., F.S.A., who was formerly in private architectural practice, is now engaged mainly upon the conservation of Scottish Ancient Monuments and Historic Buildings. He is the author of "The Architecture of Scottish Post-Reformation Churches 1560-1843". (Oxford, 1957).

ILLUSTRATIONS
The Author and Publishers gratefully acknowledge their indebtedness to:-
Ministry of Public Building and Works: Maes Howe 8, 18, Rousay, Brogar, Glenelg 10, Aileach 11, Unstan and Callanish 10, Torr a'Chaisteil, Skara Brae, Jarlshof 20, Egilsay 25, Elgin 37, Caerlaverock 45.
Royal Commission on Ancient and Historic Monuments of Scotland: Balmoral and McEwan Hall Edinburgh 17, Kirkwall 28, Stirling 51, Mellerstain and Yester 75, Taymouth 79, Avon Aqueduct 80, Bannockburn 81, Moray Place and Caledonia Road Church Glasgow 82, Grosvenor Terrace Glasgow 85.
National Museum of Antiquities of Scotland: Fendoch and Bridgeness 21, Crovie 90.
Hunterian Museum: Balmuildy 10, Antonine Wall 21.
Edinburgh University, School of Scottish Studies: N. Uist and Auchtemuchty 90.
Edinburgh Corporation, Libraries and Museums Dept.: Holyroodhouse 50.
Aerofilms Limited: Dunadd 11, Dumbarton 23.
Planair Photography: Edinburgh, 77.
Mr. R. S. Hart: Mousa 20.
Messrs. Ian G. Lindsay and Partners: Iona 35.
Mr. W. Schomberg Scott: Culzean 78.
The pictures of the Palace of Holyroodhouse 52, 64 are reproduced by gracious permission of Her Majesty the Queen.
Other photographs are by the Author and by Oriel Studios.

# ARCHITECTURE

## *of*

# SCOTLAND

by

GEORGE HAY

# ORIEL PRESS LTD

Cap.2

ISBN 0 85362 164 0

Caerlaverock Castle, Dumfriesshire, Detail 1634

Published by ORIEL PRESS LTD. (Routledge & Kegan Paul Ltd.)
Branch End, Stocksfield, Northumberland NE43 7NA
Printed and bound in Great Britain by Knight & Forster Ltd. Leeds
Text set by Northumberland Press Ltd. Gateshead, Tyne & Wear

# Contents

This book is designed for browsing in any
period, but please read pages 8 to 17
first in order to understand how it fits into
the whole history of Scottish architecture.

Inverkeithing, Fife, Market Cross 15th Century
Unicorn and Sundial 1688

# 6  Glossary

**Abutment,** solid resistance to lateral thrust of an arch

**Aisle,** part of a church separated from nave or choir by an arcade, a projecting wing or chapel

**Apse,** semi-circular or polygonal termination to a plan

**Arcade,** row of arches supported by piers or columns

**Barmkin,** defensive enclosure attached to a tower-house

**Baroque,** rich bold and vital architecture following the High Renaissance

**Barrel vault,** continuous vault of semi-circular, segmental or pointed profile

**Bretasche,** defensive timber gallery

**Buttress,** pier built against a wall to resist outward thrust

**Caponier,** stone traverse giving flanking fire along a ditch

**Chancel,** east end of main body of a church

**Clerestory,** storey with windows above adjacent roof

**Corbel,** bracket, usually of stone

**Cornice,** moulded coping of wall or entablature

**Crenellation,** battlementing with alternate voids and solids

**Crossing,** intersection of transepts and main body of a church

**Crowsteps,** stones forming stepped profile in a gable

**Cruck,** arched rafter and wall-post in timber framed building

**Cusp,** point between foils in Gothic tracery

**Donjon,** main tower in a castle

**Dormer,** vertical window in sloping roof

**Enceinte,** an enclosure

**Entablature,** upper part (architrave, frieze and cornice) of an order in classical architecture

**Forestair,** external access stair, usually of stone

**Fluting,** decorative vertical channelling

**Groin,** intersection of vault cells

**Harl, harling,** external rough-cast wall rendering

**Henge,** a pre-historic embanked sanctuary

**Hypocaust,** duct distributing hot air throughout a building

**Jamb,** side of window or door, wing of a building

**Lancet,** slender window with pointed head

**Lierne,** short intermediate rib in vaulting

**Lintel,** beam over opening

**Machicolation,** parapet corbelling with openings for dropping of missiles

**Mannerism,** modern term applied to proto-Baroque art and architecture

**Mullion,** vertical dividing member in a window

**Ogee, ogival,** having combined convex and concave curves

**Order,** a system of classical architecture comprising column with base and cap and entablature

**Oriel,** a corbelled window

**Palladian,** architectural style derived from Andrea Palladio

**Pediment,** a moulded gable in classical architecture, triangular or segmental

**Pend,** covered passage-way through a building

**Pilaster,** pillar of rectangular form attached to a wall

**Pinnacle,** spire-like termination surmounting buttress or parapet

**Quoin,** dressed external corner stone

**Rib,** projecting arched member in vaulting

**Romanesque,** architecture developed from Roman

**Screens,** service space partitioned from medieval hall

**String course,** horizontal projecting band or moulding on a wall face

**Tracery,** pattern work in stone at head of Gothic window, also applied to similar work in wood panelling

**Transept,** transverse arm of a cruciform church

**Triforium,** gallery between roof and vault of a side aisle

**Truss,** a roof frame or framed beam

**Turnpike stair,** spiral stair

**Tympanum,** panel within arch-head or pediment

**Vallum,** a rampart

**Vault,** arched covering of stone or brick

**Voussoir,** truncated wedge-shaped arch stone

# SCOTLAND

Shetland

Orkney

Caithness

Sutherland

Ross & Cromarty

Nairn-shire

Moray

Banffshire

Aberdeenshire

Kincardine-shire

Inverness-shire

Angus

Perthshire

Argyll

Fife

Kinross

Clackmannan

Stirlingshire

Dunbartonshire

Renfrewshire

W. Lothian

East Lothian

Midlothian

Berwickshire

Buteshire

Lanarkshire

Peebles-shire

Selkirk-shire

Roxburghshire

Ayrshire

Dumfriesshire

Kirkcudbright-shire

Wigtownshire

IRELAND

ENGLAND

### POST AND LINTEL

This is the simplest of architectural forms. It was the basis of the sophisticated Classical architecture of Greece and Rome. The span was limited by the dimensions of available stone lintels.

### ROUND ARCH AND VAULT

The arch made of wedge-shaped stones (voussoirs) and the barrel vault were used by both Etruscans and Romans. The latter developed the cross-vault, in effect the intersection of two barrel vaults, as well as the saucer dome to roof circular buildings.

Romanesque architecture was a development of the basic principles of Roman construction, particularly in the round arch and cross vault.

### CORBEL VAULT AND DOME

This form of construction was used in such structures as the 'Megalithic' chambered tombs of Neolithic type, the 'bee-hive' cells and oratories of early Celtic monasteries and the later shieling *bothans* in summer pastures of the Highland zone. The basic idea is a series of courses, or rings, of stones each projecting beyond the one below until the space to be covered is reduced to a small opening which can be closed by a single stone.

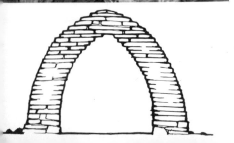

1. Maes Howe, Orkney
2. Dunfermline Abbey, Triforium
3. Corbelled Vault

POINTED ARCH AND RIBBED VAULT

These, which were developed in late Romanesque building, are the characteristic features of Gothic architecture. The separation of structural rib and pier from the infilling panels rather than the pointed arch itself is, however, what distinguishes Gothic building.

THE RENAISSANCE

Up to the Renaissance, which originated in Italy about the beginning of the fifteenth century, the character of architecture was generally expressive of the function of the building, local traditions and the materials and structural methods employed. With the Renaissance the formal values and restraint of Classical design were reasserted.

THE INDUSTRIAL AGE

The Classical ideal gave way to building methods and new structural techniques which sought to satisfy the demands of a changing society. Many styles of design were exploited, combined sometimes with decorative features of traditional form. We now see this period as one of transition and the search for an architecture expressive of a new technological civilization.

MODERN ARCHITECTURE

As in a medieval timber-framed and masonry structures, modern design is based upon the logical use of current structural forms. It seeks to reflect the potentialities of steel and reinforced concrete construction as well as the use of prefabrication, system building and new synthetic materials.

Stirling, Holy Rude Church

Edinburgh, Duddingston House
1768 by W. Chambers

Edinburgh, Royal Botanic Gardens,
Palm House 1858 by R. Matheson

Edinburgh, Scottish Widows Building
1962 by B. Spence and Partners

Rousay, Orkney, Stalled Cairn

Orkney, Ring of Brogar

The earliest and most impressive of Scottish prehistoric structures, erected about 2,000 B.C., stem from Neolithic burial rites. Great chambered tombs link with others along the west European seaboard and by implication with the distant Aegean, while so-called henge monuments and standing stones are related to the circles of Stonehenge and Avebury, and the *alignements* of Carnac.

Remains of early houses are scanty. Drystone huts survive in the Northern Isles, but elsewhere shallow foundations and post-holes recall the flimsy abodes of a sparse population. Tumbled ramparts mark the sites of Iron Age hill-top settlements, while in shallow lochs there are ruined *crannogs*, artificial islands upon which stood timber houses. Cellar-like earth houses, *souterrains*, are numerous in Angus, and in the north and west wheel-houses occur. Most imposing of all are the *brochs*, circular drystone castles peculiar to Scotland, built at the beginning of our era.

Scotland remained largely outside Roman rule, though sporadic campaigns penetrated into the north-east, and for brief periods the Lowlands south of Forth and Clyde were occupied. Roman remains, though interesting, are thus of a provincial order. There are camps, forts and roads and across the Forth-Clyde isthmus, the Antonine Wall built about A.D. 143.

Glenelg, Broch

Balmuildy, Roman Fort (model)

add, Argyll, Hill Fort
each, Garvelloch Islands, Argyll,
e-Hive Hut

The European folk migrations were reflected in Scotland by settlements of Gaelic-speaking Scots in Argyll, Teutonic-speaking Angles in the south-east and later, of Norsemen in the north and west. These eventually coalesced with the Britons and Picts to form the kingdom of Scotland, the most potent unifying factor being the Christian faith. This had a footing among the Britons by the fifth century and was further propagated by the Dalriadic Scots from Ireland.

Many earlier habitations continued in use and there were tribal hill-top citadels on sites like Dumbarton Rock, Dundurn and Dunadd. There were humbler wattle houses, and Norse dwellings of *langhus* type, and near Dunbar, there is the site of a timber hall of heroic proportions within a palisaded enclosure. Celtic monastic sites occur in Iona, Skye, the Garvelloch Islands, Brough of Deerness, North Rona, Bute and elsewhere.

Apart from the church towers of Restenneth, Abernethy and Brechin, little formal building survives but sculpture abounds. Within the Ninianic see of Galloway are upright slabs with Latin inscriptions and Christian motifs, later disc-headed crosses and the Ruthwell Cross, while at Govan, Jedburgh and St. Andrews are tomb shrines. The Pictish symbol stones and cross slabs are unique and in Iona and Islay there are high crosses of Scoto-Irish type.

Restenneth Priory, Angus, Doorway

Kildalton Cross, Islay, Argyll

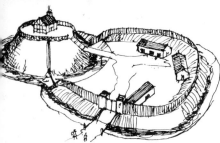

Motte and Bailey Castle
Kelso Abbey, Roxburghshire,
North West Transept

Dunfermline Abbey, Fife,
North Aisle Vaulting

# Outline

The Norman conquest of England was followed by a peaceful immigration of Anglo-Normans into Scotland. The Canmore dynasty encouraged this and so laid the foundations of a feudal society. The contemporary castle, the centre of local administration and justice, was a timber structure with defensive earthworks. The Bayeux Tapestry illustrates the classic form—a tower set on a palisaded earthen mound (motte) with a similarly enclosed courtyard (bailey) and ancillary buildings, the whole encircled by a ditch and rampart. There were variants of this but such castles are now represented merely by their earthworks.

At this time the parochial organization of the church was developed, the parish usually identified with the feudal barony and its church virtually a manorial chapel. The diocesan system was also expanded to form ultimately thirteen bishoprics each with its cathedral church. Monarchs and nobles encouraged the settlement of the religious orders and so Benedictine, Cistercian, Augustinian and other houses gradually superseded the Celtic monasteries. Conformity with the religious orthodoxy of western Europe was reflected by church buildings in the cosmopolitan Norman Romanesque style, though in the Gaelic west the influence of Hiberno-Romanesque is apparent.

As part of the royal policy many burghs were founded in this period, their communities of merchants and craftsmen being largely of Anglo-Norman and Low Country stock.

Dalmeny Church, West Lothian, c.1160

undrennan Abbey, Kirkcudbright-
hire

Glasgow Cathedral, Lower Church
below the Choir 13th Century

The massive construction of Romanesque gave way to a lighter more flexible structural system based on the pointed arch. The concentration of loads upon nodal points like piers and buttresses, with flying buttresses and pinnacles as counterpoises, facilitated lighter walling and the development of traceried windows.

A Transitional period preceded First-Pointed Gothic. A so-called Decorated phase ensued and then, as elsewhere, a form of National Gothic. Transitional and early Gothic conform with that elsewhere in Britain but Decorated work is more native in character, sometimes incorporating English and French features as at Melrose. National Gothic, unlike the airy Perpendicular of England, is somewhat dour in style. Characteristic features are flagged roofs supported on pointed tunnel vaults, apsidal ends with buttresses having numerous off-sets and square towers, with gables, spires or open masonry crowns. Persistent Celtic traditions are evident in the West Highlands where a late flowering of sculptured crosses and tomb slabs occurred.

The monasteries were fully established by 1300 as were the cathedrals, apart from later rebuildings. The friaries reached their fullest development during the fifteenth century and the same period is marked by the foundation of some forty collegiate churches, several of them extra-parochial. Most of the parish churches were in being by the end of the thirteenth century, but many of the town churches were enlarged or rebuilt during the fifteenth century.

Ladykirk, Berwickshire, c. 1500
(Tower top 1743)

Bothwell Castle, Lanarkshire,
13th Century

Borthwick Castle, Midlothian, c.1430

The first stone castles made their appearance before the end of the twelfth century; Cobbie Row's in Orkney and Castle Sween in Argyll are regarded as the earliest. The thirteenth-century norm was an enclosure of curtain walls and flanking towers, as at Bothwell or Kildrummy with the great frontal gatehouse block as a later development. In the hall-house, the *palatium* or hall rather than the tower was the dominant element but, as in Ireland, the vertical tower-house became the most characteristic feudal dwelling.

The later Middle Ages witnessed an extensive programme of reconstruction at the royal palaces of Linlithgow, Falkland, Dunfermline and Holyroodhouse and the castles of Stirling and Edinburgh. Some of these works, which were of European stature, manifest early Renaissance influences in the form of Classical details of *François Premier* type. In this respect Falkland and Stirling are outstanding. A few aristocratic dwellings belatedly reflect the influence of this court school in features like geometric stairs, dining and drawing rooms, long galleries and Classical details.

Linlithgow Palace, East Front
c. 1435

Few urban medieval buildings survive, but it was during this period that the older burghs assumed the plan forms they preserved until the Industrial Revolution and which are still apparent in towns like Edinburgh, Stirling, St. Andrews or Elgin.

Stirling Castle, Prince's Tower and Curtain Wall c.1505, Palace Block c.1540

wallan Castle, Ayrshire, 1562

inton, East Lothian, 1620

rleton Church, East Lothian,
rcherfield Aisle 1664

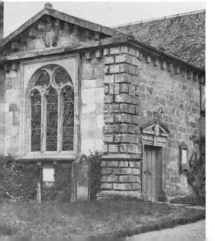

The Italian Renaissance was a reversion to Classical traditions. In Scotland, as in north-west Europe generally, the first effects of its influence show in fugitive Italianate details within a medieval context. Little developed from the Francophile royal works of the early sixteenth century, but the religious Reformation of 1560, and a consequent secularization of church wealth, gave impetus to extensive building activity among nobility and gentry. Thus the 'Baronial' castellated style, modulated both by artillery developments and by Renaissance influence, reached its zenith in the early seventeenth century.

Older churches were modified to suit the Reformed liturgy, and new ones, though modest in size, demonstrated novel plan forms as well as persistent medieval masonry traditions.

Certain royal works, public buildings and large houses, still mainly the product of master-masons, developed a formality in planning along with a pseudo-classical embellishment of Netherlands type, derived largely from continental pattern books.

The Restoration of 1660, and the advent of professional architects like Sir William Bruce and James Smith, introduced a fully developed classicism in works like the rebuilt Palace of Holyroodhouse (64) and mansions such as Kinross, Hopetoun and Melville. Meanwhile, in the burghs, stone buildings replaced earlier timber ones and in houses and tolbooths the native vernacular was combined with Dutch and Baltic features or a venturesome classicism.

Banff, Duff House c.1740 by
W. Adam, senior

Inveraray Castle, Argyll, 1745-61
by R. Morris. Dormers and Turret
Roofs 19th Century

Below left/right: Edinburgh, Moray
Place 1822 by J. G. Graham /
Glasgow, Hutcheson's Hospital
1805 by D. Hamilton

Scottish Georgian architecture assimilated much from England. The works of William Adam were in the Baroque tradition of Gibbs and Vanbrugh, but with Palladian and native overtones. The neo-Classical reaction, seen in different ways in the buildings of Chambers, the Adam brothers and Mylne, culminated in the Greek Revival. A parallel development rooted in the literary Romantic Movement and the cult of the picturesque produced a revived medieval castellated and ecclesiastical architecture of an idealized and decorative order. Authentic military building and engineering works such as roads, barracks and fortifications followed the Jacobite risings, the most impressive architecturally being Fort George.

Town architecture preserved much of its vernacular character but public buildings and houses of more sophisticated design were built within this context and as part of urban planning developments. The New Town of Edinburgh, begun in 1767, was the most outstanding of the latter but impressive neo-Classical civic architecture was also produced in Perth, Glasgow, Aberdeen and elsewhere. Improving landlords were largely responsible for the formal layout of planned new towns and villages.

The Industrial Revolution and better communications witnessed new architectural forms in mills and warehouses, industrial villages and civil engineering works like bridges and aqueducts. New farm buildings, cottages and grain mills likewise stemmed from agrarian developments.

Edinburgh, Royal College of
Physicians 1845 by T. Hamilton

The accession of Queen Victoria saw orthodox architectural thought, based largely on historicism, following either neo-Classical or Romantic lines. The former culminated in the suave Greek Revival buildings of Thomas Hamilton and W. H. Playfair and in the more individual works of Alexander ('Greek') Thomson. The Romantic school, now more antiquarian than formerly, produced houses in revived medieval styles, as well as a number of Gothic public buildings. The idiom was usually a paper-conceived rendering of exotic Perpendicular or Tudor, but, later, houses took on a somewhat metallic Scots Baronial character and churches something of native medieval tradition.

There were revivals of other British and foreign historical styles, seen at their best in Glasgow, but of greater significance were new structural techniques stimulated by rapid industrial expansion in which cast iron, steel and reinforced concrete were used. In the hands of pioneer architects and engineers novel architectural forms were evolved in structures like railway stations, bridges and warehouses.

This revolution in design and construction, the Arts and Crafts and Art Nouveau movements, including the works of Charles Rennie Mackintosh were steps towards a modern architectural idiom, which achieved common acceptance by the second World War.

2. Balmoral Castle, Aberdeenshire, 1853–56
3. Edinburgh, McEwan Hall 1890 by
   R. R. Anderson
4. East Kilbride, Lanarkshire, Shopping
   Centre 1965

Ritual monuments constitute the most impressive of early prehistoric remains. Maes Howe is the classic example of the varied collective chambered tombs erected by those Neolithic settlers who introduced agriculture and stockbreeding during the third millenium B.C. Burial customs varied; inhumation and cremation were both practised. Barrows and cairns covering one or more individual cists developed in Bronze Age times, as did collective cemeteries. Circular open air ditch-enclosed sanctuaries were also devised, some with standing monoliths as at Brogar and Stenness or boulders like Torhouse. Some groups like the circle and avenue of Callanish are associated with burial cairns or cists. Contemporaneous are the mysterious 'cup-and-ring' carvings found on rock outcrops and occasionally on monoliths and burial cists.

Throughout the country, hut circles, postholes and hearths are the sole traces of early timber and wattle houses which were often grouped within an enclosure. In the Northern Isles, ·the drystone settlements of Skara Brae, Rinyo and Jarlshof survive as petrified impressions of the vanished timber abodes of other areas. The aisled round house and the wheelhouse are clearly derived from timber prototypes. *Crannogs*, circular timber houses reared upon artificial islands, are numerous in the south-west and cellar-like *souterrains* in Angus.

Unstan Chambered Cairn, Orkney

Torhouse Circle, Wigtownshire

Callanish Circle, Lewis, Ross and Cromarty

Above left:   Torr a' Chaisteil, Arran
Above right:  Skara Brae, Orkney

Jarlshof, Shetland

Mousa Broch, Shetland

With the Iron Age settlement of the Celts, defensive structures predominate. Fortified farmsteads and great hill-top settlements like Kaimes, Traprain Law and the Caterthuns, were built with defensive earthworks and walls which were sometimes timber-laced, recalling the *murus Gallicus* seen by Caesar in Gaul. The *brochs* of the north, the most spectacular of Scottish Iron Age works bring us to the threshold of history. Related to them are galleried duns and forts of various forms and confusing classifications.

Typical broch plan,
Dun Troddan,
Glenelg

# Roman

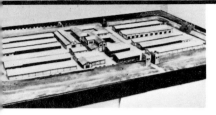

ndoch, Roman Fort (model

ntonine Wall (model)

Unlike southern Britain, where an urban Roman society left considerable remains, Scotland was partially and briefly occupied, first during Flavian times from about A.D. 50 to 100 and again in the Antonine period from about 140 to the end of that century. Roman monuments are thus of a frontier nature and include bases and camps, roads and signal stations.

Marching camps mark the routes of various campaigns, probably the earliest being that of Agricola who, about A.D. 80, defined the frontier across the Forth-Clyde isthmus by a chain of forts. This was more firmly established about A.D. 143 when Lollius Urbicus built the Antonine Wall. Mainly of turf on a stone base with a ditch outside and a military way within, it was uneasily garrisoned in some twenty forts along its length until about the end of the second century.

Roman sites on both sides of the frontier have been identified and investigated. In the south the most considerable forts are Birrens near the Solway and Newstead on the Tweed, while in the north Ardoch and Inchtuthill are the most impressive. Such forts followed formal rectangular plans, enclosed by ditches and ramparts with the principal buildings of stone heated by a hypocaust system. Archeological 'finds' include weapons, domestic articles and stone altars, distance slabs from the Antonine Wall and a buried horde of silver plate from Traprain Law in East Lothian.

Antonine Wall, Bridgeness Distance Slab

# Dark Ages

During the so-called Dark Ages much of the population continued to inhabit earlier dwellings. *Brochs, duns, wheel-houses, crannogs* and the like were doubtless occupied into medieval times. There is evidence of the re-occupation of some Iron Age sites as well as the establishment of tribal *oppida* like Dumbarton, Dunadd (11), Dundurn and Dunollie. There were many dun-like structures and ring and promontary forts of stone, but much building was of timber which has perished leaving scant traces. Truly monumental must have been the great timber hall and other structures on Doon Hill near Dunbar, resembling in character Saxon work at Yeavering.

Celtic monasteries founded by Dalriadic missionaries are now represented by the traces of bee-hive cells with one or more chapels and other communal buildings within a circular *cashel* or rampart, like the Irish chieftain's *rath*, though the Columbian monastery of Iona had an unusual rectangular *vallum*. At Aileach in the Garvelloch Islands are remains of bee-hive huts (11) and other structures, while at Brough of Deerness the buildings were mainly rectangular.

By the end of the eight century the Norsemen appeared, first as marauders and later as settlers. Remains of their dwellings, *langhus* structures of stone, survive at Birsay, Jarlshof, Freswick and elsewhere. Mounds cover their graves which in a few cases were boat burials.

Dumbarton Rock

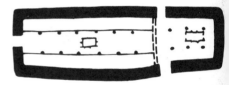

Typical *langhus* plan, based on Jarlshot

Left: Whithorn, Wigtownshire, Cross Slab
Right: Ruthwell Church, Dumfriesshire, Cross

Examples of formal architecture are few. The square tower of Restenneth, part of which is of archaic pre-Norman Romanesque character (11), dates from the period following the Pictish conformity with the Roman church in 710. At Brechin and Abernethy we find round towers of Irish type, the former a tenth-century construction, and the upper part of the latter a twelfth-century reconstruction.

The rich legacy of Dark Age sculpture is one with the culture of the Kells and Lindisfarne gospels, and the metallurgical genius of the Ardagh chalice and the Monymusk reliquary. The rough tombstones of Kirkmadrine and Whithorn with incised cross, *Chi-rho* and Latin names are of 5th-7th century date, and also to Galloway belong disc-head crosses of the 9th-11th centuries. The Ruthwell Cross of *c*.700 is the finest product of Northumbrian art. To this amalgam of Irish and Continental traditions, belong shrine fragments at Jedburgh and St. Andrews, the Govan sarcophagus and sundry slabs and cross shafts. The Pictish sculptures developed from rough seventh-century monoliths, with incised animals and symbols, to relief work with symbols and cross, and finally to cross-slabs without symbols but with features of Northumbrian derivation. High crosses of Scoto-Irish type occur at Islay (11) and Iona; fragments at the latter show mortice and tenon construction, suggestive of vanished timber prototypes.

1.   Kirkinner, Wigtownshire, Cross
2./3. Aberlemno, Angus, Cross Slab / Detail
        of reverse side

# Romanesque

ruchtag Motehill, Wigtownshire

gilsay, Orkney, Church of
St. Magnus

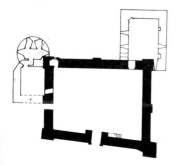

Castle Sween, Argyll, Plan

Early motte and bailey castles which marked the establishment of Anglo-Norman feudalism are now represented by earthworks like the Mote of Urr or the Bass of Inverurie. Some were subsequently crowned by stone structures, as at Duffus where results were disastrous, or otherwise incorporated into later medieval castles, as at Huntly. The characteristic Norman keep of England is unknown in Scotland, unless we accept the possibility that St. Margaret's Chapel in Edinburgh Castle formed part of one. Cobbie Row's castle of *c.*1145 survives as the stump of a small rectangular tower within defensive earthworks, but the contemporary Castle Sween in Argyll is a rectangular 'shell keep' with pilaster buttresses and later additions.

As we have seen, Romanesque churches existed in Scotland before the Anglo-Norman ecclesiastical expansion of the twelfth century. On Brough of Birsay, the lower walls of Earl Thorfinn's minster of *c.*1055 still survive, and in Orkney also is the roofless church of Egilsay, comprising chancel, nave and round tower, which could have been the scene of St. Magnus' martyrdom in 1116. Below the nave of Dunfermline are the walls of Queen Margaret's church, a composite structure fully developed by *c.*1075, whose plan is resembled by that of St. Rule's, the first priory church of St. Andrews.

St. Andrews, Fife, Priory Church of St. Rule 11th Century (Northumbrian influence)

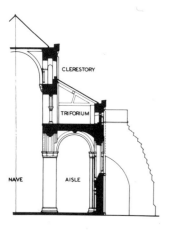

The greater Anglo-Norman churches followed English and Continental models of cruciform plan with side aisles, but Kelso (12) had a unique Rhenish arrangement with east and west transepts. Aisles were vaulted but main roofs were normally of timber, though at Kirkwall, high vaults were added to choir and nave before completion. Like Dunfermline, the east coast churches reflect the character of the Durham school, with some reminiscence of Trondheim in the transepts of Kirkwall, while the unusual choir arcades of Jedburgh have parallels at Romsey and Oxford. In Strathclyde, surviving Norman capitals at Bothwell, Douglas and Rutherglen, some of them Corinthianesque, suggest another line of Anglo-French influence and at Whithorn and Iona there are doorways in unmistakable Hiberno-Romanesque idiom.

The average parish church was an aisleless two-chamber structure, though some had tall west towers as at Dunning and Muthill and apsidal sanctuaries like Tyninghame, Dalmeny (12) or Leuchars. At Orphir, in Orkney, are the remains of a circular church with shallow apse. The Lowland churches have walling of cubical ashlar, but those of the north are of local rubble with little architectural detail. Typical features are round arches, often with chevrons and other enrichments, cylindrical piers, capitals of cushion, scallop or Corinthianesque form, and corbels carved as grotesque masks, while in doorway tympana and other focal points, sculptured subjects were drawn from Scripture or the medieval Bestiaries.

Dunfermline Abbey, Section (buttresses 1620–25)

euchars Church, Fife, Chancel c.1185

Douglas, Lanarkshire, Capital 12th Century

yninghame Church, East Lothian, 12th Century
Plan

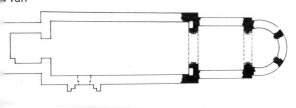

Dunfermline
Abbey,
Nave c.1150

Jedburgh
Abbey,
Choir
c.1150

Dunning
Church,
Perthshire,
late 12th
Century

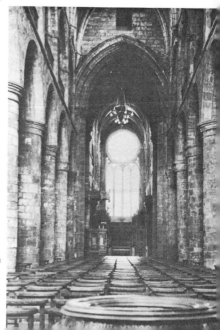

Kirkwall
Cathedral,
Orkney, 12th
and 13th
Centuries

# Gothic

There grew out of Romanesque the architecture now called Gothic which, when fully developed, enabled churches to be designed as masonry frames supporting vaulted roofs and glazed walls. This Gothic genius, however, was more than an adroit management of structural elements. The great churches of western Christendom were as functional in design as the layout of the monasteries or the defensive features of the castles. The basic impulse was given by the Church, whose well-defined doctrines, rites, and settled iconography, provided a consistent theme for architecture and the visual arts.

The Transitional phase is distinguished from Norman Romanesque by a refinement of proportion and delicacy of detail seen in features like pointed arches alongside round ones and carved capitals of water-leaf type. It is well exemplified by the nave of Jedburgh in contrast with the earlier choir and by the abbeys of Dundrennan (13) and Arbroath.

The early thirteenth century saw the advent of fully developed Gothic with its pointed arches and vaulting system; lancet windows either in single lights, grouped or with simple traceries, deep profiled mouldings and celery-like leaf work. This First-Pointed Gothic, which represents the high noon of medieval structural design, is seen at its best in the cathedrals of Glasgow, Elgin and Dunblane (37, 38) and the nave of Holyrood Abbey.

1. Jedburgh Abbey, Nave c. 1200
2. Glasgow Cathedral, Choir 13th Century
3. St. Monance Church, Fife c. 1370

Above: Melrose Abbey, Roxburghshire, South
Transept early 15th Century
Right: Edinburgh, St. Giles', Choir Vaulting
c. 1460

The Wars of Independence and consequent national exhaustion permitted little serious building during the fourteenth century until near its end. The emphasis then was on reconstruction as at Melrose, where the abbey church was rebuilt after destruction by Richard II in 1385. This work typifies the Decorated phase, with features like lierne vaults, flying buttresses and naturalistic sculpture, French-like aisle chapels and flamboyant tracery, as well as English Perpendicular windows of the York school. The same style on a minor scale is seen at Lincluden.

Seton Church, East Lothian, Choir Vaulting
c. 1480

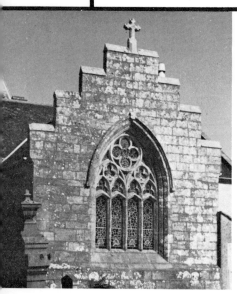

Above left: Straiton Church,
Ayrshire, c.1500
Above right: Arbuthnott Church,
Kincardineshire, c.1500
Below: Linlithgow, St Michael's
Church, Apse c.1530

During the late fifteenth and early sixteenth centuries, the last phase of Scots Gothic occurs mainly in secular churches like the cathedral naves of Aberdeen and Dunkeld, town kirks enlarged or rebuilt by rich burghers and collegiate churches founded principally by aristocratic patrons. Though in some instances there was an effort to resuscitate the spirit of thirteenth-century work, as in the Blacader aisle at Glasgow (38), this national style is marked by an almost Romanesque masculinity and features like cylindrical piers, looped window tracery often without cusps, fireproof construction in the form of tunnel vaults overlaid with stone flags, as well as fortress-like towers. The contemporary church buildings at Iona, Oronsay and Rodel, and the West Highland sculptured crosses and tomb slabs in which late Gothic details are combined with earlier Celtic tracery and leaf-work, belong to a distinctive Scoto-Irish and Gaelic context.

The Scottish monasteries which superseded earlier Celtic settlements are comparable with those of England and the Continent. They follow standard European layout, with church and living quarters disposed around a rectangular cloister, planned in detail to suit the life and rule of their respective orders. Most were founded during the twelfth century and reached their fullest development during the next. Sweetheart Abbey, a 1273 Cistercian foundation, is one of the few with extensive fourteenth-century work. Later building periods, as seen at Melrose and Crossraguel, the nave of Paisley and the chapter houses of Dundrennan and Glenluce (36) represent reconstructions. The larger monastic churches were of orthodox cruciform plan, though few were fully vaulted as at Holyrood, and some were simple aisleless buildings like Beauly and Crossraguel.

Dryburgh Abbey, Roxburghshire, Chapter House Doorway c.1200

Sweetheart Abbey, Kirkcudbright-shire, 14th Century

Inchmahome Priory, Perthshire, 13th Century

Jedburgh Abbey, Roxburghshire, c.1150–1200

In most cases the claustral buildings have suffered much destruction but those of Inchcolm survive completely roofed around an Irish-like cloister. The whole complex of Iona Abbey, a modest Benedictine foundation, is virtually complete having been largely restored in recent times. There is an unusual cloister arcade at Oronsay and portions of others exist at Glenluce and Inchmahome. The Franciscan friary of Elgin was admirably restored in 1896 as a modern convent, while in South Queensferry the choir and tower of a Carmelite friary church remain in use. Characteristic precinct walls and gateways are impressively seen at Arbroath and St. Andrews and there are fragments at Pluscarden Priory and Sweetheart Abbey.

Chapter House 13th and 14th Centuries

Left: Cloister 14th Century

Refectory late 14th Century

# Gothic

## IONA ABBEY, ARGYLL,
### 13th Century – c.1500 and later

Cloister (reconstructed)

...construction

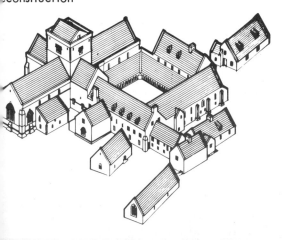

Iona Abbey, Refectory (restored)

Elgin, Greyfriars' Church 15th Century,
restored 1896

Melrose Abbey, Cloister Wall
Arcading early 15th Century

Glenluce Abbey, Chapter House 15th Century

# Gothic

Scotland's thirteen medieval cathedrals, with the exception of Elgin, Glasgow and St. Andrews, conform in size with Irish and Scandinavian rather than English standards. They were secular establishments save at St. Andrews and Whithorn, which were priory churches, and at Iona, where the abbey church became the cathedral of the Isles about 1500.

Eight were of cruciform plan with a central tower, Glasgow, Elgin and Aberdeen having in addition paired western ones. Glasgow is notable for its vaulted lower church (13) under the choir and Elgin, when fully developed, had French-like double aisles to its nave. Modest Lismore consisted merely of west tower, nave and aisleless choir and aisleless choirs also occur at Brechin, Dornoch, Dunblane, Dunkeld and Fortrose. Frequently, as at Glasgow, the high roofs of nave, choir and transepts were of timber. Dunblane is wholly without vaulting save in its Lady Chapel, while the nave at Aberdeen, a granite structure whose west front has all the militant character of Albi Cathedral in France, has an oak ceiling. Those cathedrals still in use show little of their former liturgical arrangements but Glasgow retains its fine stone *pulpitum*, or choir screen, and Dunblane some of its choir stalls.

1. Elgin Cathedral, East End 13th Century
2. Dunblane Cathedral, Nave 13th Century

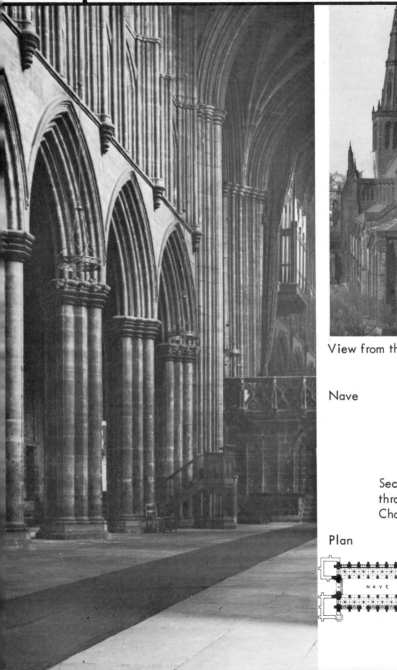

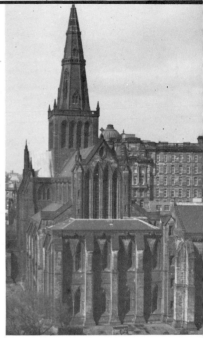

View from the East

Nave

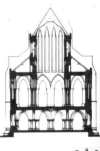

Section
through
Choir

Plan

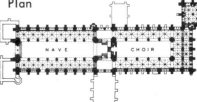

# Gothic

---

# Gothic

# Gothic

Dunkeld Cathedral, Nave early 15th Century

Dunblane Cathedral, Choir Stalls c.1500

Aberdeen, St. Machar's Cathedral, Nave Ceiling c.1520

Aberdeen, St. Machar's Cathedral, West Front c.1430, Spires c.1530

## PARISH AND COLLEGIATE CHURCHES

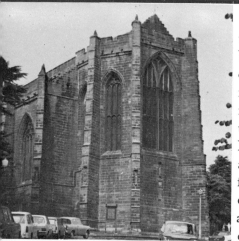

Stirling, Holy Rude Church
c.1450 – c.1540
Dundee, Tower mid–15th Century

After tremendous parochial expansion during the previous century, few parish churches were built during the thirteenth. In rural areas, a two-chamber nave and chancel structure was common, as at Abdie, but gradually a narrow gabled rectangle became the medieval norm. Typical thirteenth century examples occur at Temple, Dunstaffnage and Skipness. Wholesale monastic appropriation of parishes was the main reason for this architectural austerity. The towns which constituted single parishes, were served by more ambitious churches. The thirteenth-century church of Crail has an aisled nave, a chancel and a west tower. By reason of frequent enlargement and addition of chantry chapels, many of the town churches, by the late fifteenth and early sixteenth centuries, rivalled in size some of the cathedrals. Typical examples still in use are those of Edinburgh (St. Giles'), Linlithgow, Perth, Stirling and St. Andrews. St. Giles', Edinburgh (31), has a splendid tower with an open masonry crown as had formerly the towers of Haddington and Linlithgow: at Dundee, there is a massive structure which was intended to be similarly finished. Elsewhere austere unbuttressed towers capped by parapets and squat stone spire, or a gabled roof, are common.

Linlithgow, St. Michael's
Church c.1450 – c.1530,
Plan

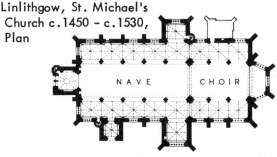

NAVE     CHOIR

## PARISH AND COLLEGIATE CHURCHES

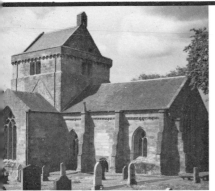

Above: Edinburgh, Corstorphine Collegiate Church 15th Century
1. Crichton Collegiate Church, Midlothian, mid-15th Century
2. Seton Collegiate Church, East Lothian, 1470 – c.1540
3. Dumfries, Lincluden Collegiate Church c.1415

Collegiate churches, some forty in number, served by staffs of secular priests, represent a late development. Founded mainly by aristocratic patrons to perform the daily offices and offer masses for the founders and their families, they varied greatly in form and size. A few of the more ambitious were never completed. Some were establishments set up in parish churches like Bothwell or Crichton, while others were extra-parochial as at Corstorphine or Roslin. The last, though small and incomplete, is unique. The town kirks of Aberdeen, Edinburgh and Haddington, served by numerous chaplains, achieved collegiate status, and the collegiate churches of St. Salvator at St. Andrews and King's College at Aberdeen, were university foundations. Architecturally such churches exemplify the last phase of Scots Gothic.

# Gothic

Roslin Collegiate Church,
Midlothian, c.1450

The plan is suggestive of Iberian
origins, for the nave was intended
in width to comprehend that of
choir and choir aisles, as at Gerona,
Spain. Further indication of this is
in the appearance of cactus leaves
in the carved lintels between the
aisle vaults.

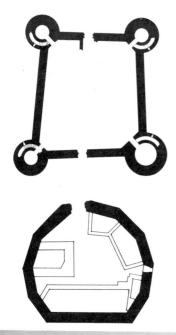

The essential feature of early stone castles is the curtain wall—a transmuted palisade—enclosing an area whose size and shape were determined by the site and within which stone or timber buildings were raised. Such are the castles of Loch Doon and Rothesay, the last a great circular 'shell-keep' with later towers and gatehouse.

Developments in siege warfare and military engineering are reflected in the larger castles of *enceinte*. Within the usual fosse and earthworks, curtain walls rose to machicolated and crenellated parapets or to timber *bretasches*, while round towers at salient points in the circuit provided enfilade defence. The lord's lodging was in one of the towers, as at Bothwell (14), Kildrummy and Inverlochy and the entrance was tunnelled through a strong gatehouse. As in some of the Edwardian Welsh castles, the gatehouse dwelling gradually superseded the donjon lodging and became a dominant feature. This development, seen at Caerlaverock and Dirleton, culminated in great symmetrical façade compositions of gatehouse, curtains and flanking towers as at Tantallon and Stirling. Eventually, as at Doune (c.1380), a great front block contained most of the essential accommodation, lesser elements being disposed around the courtyard behind.

1. Rothesay Castle, Bute, 13th Century
2. Inverlochy Castle, Inverness–shire, 13th Century, Plan
3. Loch Doon Castle, Ayrshire, c.1300, Plan
4. Tantallon Castle, East Lothian, 14th Century

# Medieval

Above: Caerlaverock Castle, Dumfriesshire
13th and 15th Centuries
Right: Dirleton Castle, East Lothian, 13th
and 14th Centuries
Below: Kildrummy Castle, Aberdeenshire,
13th Century, Plan

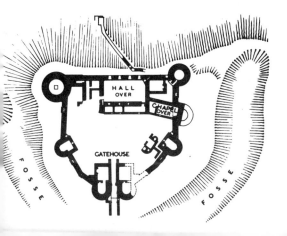

A type of feudal dwelling having lengthy antecedents is the hall-house, in which the hall, usually at first-floor level, is the dominant component, the lord's quarters being at one end sometimes in a tower. The best surviving examples are Morton, Rait and Tulliallan; but, at Kirkwall, the thirteenth-century Bishop's Palace, which recalls Håkonshall in Bergen, is incorporated in later building. Craigie has the remains of fine ribbed groin vaulting and, incorporated in its external walls, an earlier crenellated parapet. This form of dwelling was doubtless the basis for the many moated manor-houses of timber which were a feature of medieval times, but of which no example survives. In many cases extensions within a tower-house *barmkin* produced an informal courtyard dwelling as at Castle Campbell, Craigmillar and Edzell.

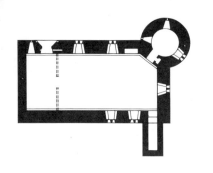

1. Doune Castle, Perthshire, c.1380
2. Typical hall-house plan, Rait Castle, Nairnshire, early 14th Century
3. Craigie Castle, Ayrshire, c.1400

Below: Hermitage Castle, Roxburghshire, 14th and 15th Centuries

By far the most numerous of Scots castles are tower-houses, in which all the elements—stores, kitchen, hall, chamber and bedrooms—were set on end, served by one or more turnpike stairs as vertical corridors. This most compact of defensive dwellings, with wide variations of size and plan form, was built by small laird and great baron alike, and became something of a symbol of feudal jurisdiction. There was usually a *barmkin* or courtyard with ancillary buildings but in some cases there is no evidence of this. There are modest rectangular towers like Liberton as well as massive ones like Comlongan, Carrick and Threave with numerous mural chambers. A *jamb*, or wing, sometimes containing the stair, produced an L-plan as in Craigmillar and Neidpath, while unique in respect of size and form is Borthwick (14) which is of rectangular U-plan. Floor construction generally alternated between timber joists and stone barrel vaults, though in a few cases like Auchindoun and Towie Barclay ribbed groin vaults occur. Pitched roofs, frequently covered with stone flags, rose within corbelled parapets which, at external angles, developed into projecting rounds elaborately corbelled.

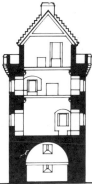

1. Comlongon Tower, Dumfriesshire, c.1450
2. Typical tower-house section, Fatlips Castle, Roxburghshire, 16th Century

Left: Edinburgh, Craigmillar Castle, Machicolations 15th Century

The royal palace of Linlithgow is a fifteenth-century courtyard composition, defensive but designed with an eye to dignity and domestic convenience. The main rooms are on the first floor, the royal apartments to the west and south-west, the chapel in the south range and, on the east, the great hall, or 'Lion Chamber', which rivalled that of Stirling as the finest state apartment in the realm.

At the castles of Edinburgh and Stirling, the buildings were concentrated for defensive reasons at the entrance on the east end of their respective rocks, the palace quarters being disposed around upper closes behind. Edinburgh has been much altered but its great hall (c.1505) has early Renaissance corbels supporting an open timber roof. At Stirling, the great hall, though mutilated, survives with tall vaulted bay windows flanking its dais, while the adjoining palace is an outstanding c.1540 essay in the manner of *François Premier*. Its French master-masons came from Falkland Palace where they had built the gatehouse and south and east ranges in much the same style.

Courtyard 15th Century

Gateway c.1535

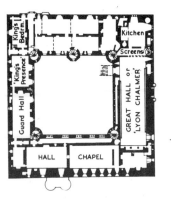

Plan 15th-16th Centuries, North Quarter 1618-21

Edinburgh Castle, Great Hall
c.1505

Stirling Castle, Gatehouse c.1505 (19th Century
crenellations)

The medieval castle was transformed by the development of gunpowder. Gun loops took the place of arrow slits and, in tower-houses, *jambs*, sometimes contrived at diagonally opposite corners to facilitate covering small arms fire, produced the so-called Z-plan and fascinating geometric forms. High curtains and crenellated towers gave way to lower thicker walls, gun platforms and embrasures as at Ravenscraig (*c.*1465) and the later Half Moon Bastion at Edinburgh; while at Craignethan the west curtain of the inner courtyard is fronted by a great ditch which was covered by raking fire from the loops of a traverse and a vaulted *caponier*. Later castles are characterized by decorative details like corbelling, corner turrets and the like derived from former defensive features.

Falkland Palace, Fife, Gatehouse Tower c.1540

Dunfermline Palace, 14th and 16th Centuries. (Abbey seen behind)

Right: Edinburgh, Palace of Holyroodhouse,
after Gordon of Rothiemay, 1647

The royal palace of Dunfermline grew out of the
fourteenth century guesthouse of the Benedictine
abbey, which was adapted for the purpose, and a
similar origin accounts for the early sixteenth
century 'fair palice' and 'greit toure' of James V
at Holyrood. Only the tower survives, incorporated in the late seventeenth century rebuilding.

To appreciate Scottish architectural developments from the sixteenth century onwards, some knowledge of the Italian Renaissance is necessary.

Fifteenth-century Italy experienced a revival of interest in Classical antiquity and its arts and architecture. Roman architectural prototypes were interpreted with some freedom and the writings of scholar architects provided basic principles. The early Renaissance work of Florence gave way to the Rome-centred High Renaissance. A Mannerist phase ensued, in which subtle aesthetic artifice took the place of earlier imitativeness; it was then followed by Baroque flamboyance.

After their Italian campaigns between 1495 and 1525, French monarchs enticed Italian artists to France with obvious architectural consequences. Buildings of the northern Italian provinces, like the Certosa at Pavia, appealed particularly to French patrons. Traditional Franco-Scottish ties and the marriage of James V to Mary of Lorraine which brought about an influx of French craftsmen, infused Scottish building with something of *François Premier* mannerisms.

Florence, S. Lorenzo 1421–60
Pavia, The Certosa begun 1491
St. Andrews, Fife, St. Mary's College, Corbel c.1545
Stirling Castle, Ceiling Boss c.1540

The first Scottish evidences of the Renaissance are seen in Italianate details absorbed into the yet medieval repertoire of painter, carver and master-mason. In some royal works where Frenchmen were employed the style of *Francois Premier* predominates. The great halls of Edinburgh and Stirling castles are characteristic Gothic structures with Classical details. The fountain at Linlithgow Palace is a florid Gothic work with flying buttresses and Renaissance medallions. The palaces of Falkland and Stirling are more advanced. At the former, the courtyard elevations have buttresses devised as engaged Classical columns and there are paired medallion heads in each bay. At Stirling, the conventional suites of King's and Queen's Guard-hall, 'Presence' and Bedroom range at first-floor level around a court. The outside elevations have windows alternating with shallow arched recesses with sculptured figures upon baluster shafts. These are of French derivation as are the carved oak medallion heads which once adorned the ceiling of the King's 'Presence'. The oak ceilings at Holyroodhouse, *c.*1559, have a similar origin.

Falkland Palace, Fife, South Range c.1540

Stirling Castle, Palace Block c.1540

Edinburgh, Holyroodhouse, Oak Ceiling c.1559

The influence of this 'court school' is seen in the niche details of St. Mary's College, St. Andrews, and in 'Mar's Wark', Stirling, the town lodging of the Earl of Mar, begun about 1570. Something of the style of the Loire is evident in Archbishop Hamilton's facade at St. Andrews Castle, in the Regent Morton's gateway at Edinburgh Castle and in the great oriels of the Bishop's Palace, Kirkwall. Even more emphatically French is the ornate cresting of corbelled oriels, dormers and chimney-heads, dated 1602, on the palace block of Huntly Castle.

There is a 1566 rusticated doorway of Italianate design in Edinburgh Castle and of clear Italian or Iberian provenance is the *c.*1590 north quarter of Crichton Castle, while the Chapel Royal at Stirling (1594) has a Classical doorway with flanking columns. Increasing Renaissance influence is also seen in a certain formality in planning and in the Classical ornaments of painted ceilings, plasterwork and woodwork.

Edinburgh Castle, Doorway 1566

Stirling, Mar's Wark 1572

Stirling Castle, Chapel Royal 1594

Edinburgh Castle, Regent Morton's Gateway 1574

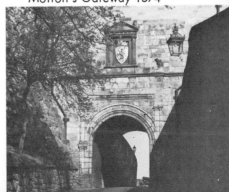

Delgaty Castle, Aberdeenshire, Painted Ceiling 1597

Above left: Crichton Castle, Midlothian, North Quarter c.1590

Huntly Castle, Palace Block 1602

Burntisland Church, Fife, 1592, Upper Tower 1749

The Reformation of 1560, a stringent economy and a Calvinist theology and liturgy resulted in the modification of medieval churches and in the building of new ones of novel form combined with conservative masonry traditions. Notable among the few sixteenth-century examples is Burntisland (1592), a square-towered structure with galleries and a central floor space for the long communion tables of the Reformed rite. Other centrally planned buildings are the seventeenth-century Greek cross churches of Fenwick, Kirkintilloch, Thurso and Lauder, the last by Bruce.

Rural churches generally followed the medieval rectangular plan as at Lyne and Dirleton, which has a west tower, but the addition of a transeptal aisle, often with a laird's loft and burial place, produced a T-plan. This became a classic Scottish type of which Ayr, Careston and Pitsligo are characteristic examples. Some T-kirks instead of the normal gable belfry have towers either at the west end like Anstruther Easter and Polwarth or on the long side as at Carrington, Yester or the Tron, Edinburgh.

Right: Anstruther Easter Church, Fife, 1634–44

Pitsligo Church, Aberdeenshire, Laid's Loft 1634

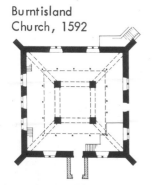

Burntisland Church, 1592

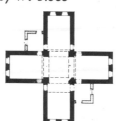

Lauder Church, Berwickshire, 1673 by W. Bruce

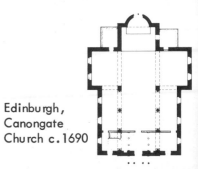

Edinburgh, Canongate Church c. 1690

Greyfriars, Edinburgh (1620), originally a large aisled Gothic church with west tower, was enlarged in 1722 after the destruction of its west end by an explosion. The Canongate, Edinburgh (c.1690) has a Baroque aisled cruciform plan which may be explained by the Catholicism of its designer James Smith and his patron James VII. Smith too seems to have been responsible for the unusual church of Durisdeer, a classical T-plan building with a Baroque mausoleum to the north, and laird's rooms and a tower at the west end.

Architecturally, such churches, in the main, display a vernacular austerity with harled walls, masonry details like moulded doorways, windows often of Gothic form, ornamental belfries or towers with ogival heads or balustrades and spires. A strange revived Gothic was used by Archbishop Spottiswoode at his model church of Dairsie in 1621. Elsewhere the Netherlandish Classical idiom was employed as in the Tron, Edinburgh, and followed by more sophisticated Renaissance details.

Edinburgh, Canongate Church c.1690 by J. Smith

Left: Edinburgh, Greyfriars' Church 1620 and 1722

Polwarth Church, Berwickshire, 1703

# Scots Baronial

MIDMAR CASTLE,
ABERDEENSHIRE, c. 1570

**16th and 17th CENTURIES**

ellie Castle, Fife, 1573–1606
astle Fraser, Aberdeenshire,
576–1617

The English invasions of 1545 and 1547 and the secularization of church wealth at the Reformation of 1560 gave considerable impetus to domestic building. Castellated architecture enjoyed a brief but brilliant Indian summer reaching its peak during the early seventeenth century. In this so-called 'Baronial' phase, new buildings and additions to earlier ones are marked by a patent pacification of one-time defensive features and a venturesome use of Classical details. Corbelled upper storeys recall earlier machicolated parapets and pepper-pot turrets defensive corner rounds; new details like pedimented dormers and wall-head balustrades entered the vocabulary. Defence was not, however, forgotten as shot-holes, stout doors, iron *yetts* and window grilles testify. These are found in structures of subtle geometrical forms with slated roofs and virile masonry contrasting with harled walls.

Most typical are the kindred north-east castles of Craigievar, Crathes, Fraser and Midmar, Glamis and Claypotts in Angus and Amisfield in Dumfriesshire. Fyvie is a swagger, symmetrical composition incorporating earlier work, as is Craigston. Tower-houses, commonly of traditional rectangular, L or Z-plans, maintained their vogue, and include such diverse examples as Carnasserie, Gogar and diminutive Coxton.

Contemporary with such castellated essays are admirable lairds' houses of more domestic character. Northfield (61) has corner turrets but others like Ford, Peffermill and the manse of Anstruther Easter retain only a stair tower.

Crathes
Castle,
Kincard-
ineshire,
c.1595

Amisfield
Tower,
Dumfries-
shire,
1600

Fyvie Castle,
Aberdeenshire,
c.1600

Above: Craigievar Castle, Aberdeenshire, 1626
Above left: Coxton Tower, Moray, 1644
Below left: Pathhead, Midlothian, Ford House
   1680
Below: Northfield, East Lothian, 1611

Contemporaneously with early seventeenth-century 'Baronial' structures, certain royal works, public buildings and houses were designed in a pseudo-Classical manner, now loosely termed 'Jacobean'. This Renaissance mannerism, cradled in the Low Countries, was common to all north-west Europe. It is mainly made up from formal plans derived from the publications of Serlio, Vignola and others, ornamental details from Low Country pattern books and native masonry traditions.

The King's Lodging in Edinburgh Castle (1615-17) and the north quarter of Linlithgow Palace (1618-21) are rebuildings by William Wallace with features like pedimented windows and ogival-headed turrets. The east range of Caerlaverock Castle (1634) is a similar development.

Above right: Linlithgow Palace, North Quarter, 1618–21

Below right: Caerlaverock Castle, Dumfriesshire, East Quarter 1634

Below: Edzell Castle, Angus, Walled Garden 1604

Heriot's Hospital in Edinburgh (1628-59), the work successively of William Wallace, William Ayton and John Mylne is an ambitious courtyard composition with corner towers; and over the entrance there is a steeple designed by Robert Mylne in 1693. It has a complete repertoire of characteristic turrets, buckle quoins and carved 'doodles'. The now vanished College of Glasgow was equally impressive and to the same school belong the Parliament Hall in Edinburgh, Cowane's Hospital in Stirling, Linlithgow Tolbooth and the steeples of the Merchants' Hall and Tolbooth in Glasgow.

Characteristic houses, usually with fine plasterwork and decorative painting are Pinkie (1613), Winton (15) by William Wallace, Innes (1640-53) by William Ayton, Pitreavie and Hills. Notable town mansions are Argyll Lodging, Stirling (73), and Moray House, Edinburgh (c.1630). To the same tradition belong the wellhead at Pinkie, and the walled gardens at Edzell Castle (1604) and Aberdour.

Edinburgh, Heriot's Hospital
1628–59, Tower c.1693

Plan of Heriot's Hospital

CHAPEL — COUNCIL ROOM — DINING HALL — KIT-CHEN

Edinburgh, Parliament Hall
1632–41

**Stirling, Cowane's Hospital 1636–49**

# Scots Renaissance

PALACE OF HOLYROODHOUSE
1671 – 78 by W. Bruce

**16th to 18th CENTURY**

inburgh, Palace of Holyroodhouse, ntrance 1671–78 by W. Bruce

The Cromwellian occupation was notable mainly at Holyroodhouse for destruction, and at Ayr, Inverlochy, Inverness, Leith, Perth and elsewhere for fortifications some fragments of which have survived.

The Restoration of 1660 initiated a busy building period during which a fully developed Renaissance classicism was established. As in sixteenth-century essays like Craignethan and Earl's Palace, Birsay, some formal planning was attempted using vernacular elements. This was done by Sir William Bruce in the enlargement of Balcaskie, Brunstane and Thirlestane and by James Smith at Traquair. A more advanced idiom appeared, however, in the reconstruction of the Palace of Holyroodhouse, which was started in 1671, with Bruce as Surveyor and Robert Mylne as Master Mason. A symmetrical west façade was devised incorporating the early sixteenth-century tower, as a metamorphosis of the medieval defensive front originally envisaged by James V. The state apartments are disposed in three pilastered storeys of successive Doric, Ionic and Corinthian orders around a chaste 'piazza'. The French refinement, doubtless the result of Bruce's travels, is apparent in his other palatial work, Hopetoun (67), built 1699 to 1702, and enlarged by William Adam.

The Classicism initiated by Holyroodhouse influenced many lesser houses and was interestingly combined with vernacular elements in buildings like Caroline Park in Edinburgh and Brucefield in Stirlingshire.

2. Traquair House, Peeblesshire, Gates c.1700
3. Edinburgh, Caroline Park, South Front 1696

Kinross, Kinross House c.1686–91 by W. Bruce.
South–West Front and Gateway

Bruce's own Kinross House (*c.*1686-91) is an advanced Renaissance *palazzo* to which are related his Mertoun and Moncreiffe, the latter burnt out about 1960. His Auchendinny (1707) is a small rectangular house linked by curved screen walls to pavilion blocks, an arrangement much favoured by later Palladians. Prestonfield House reflects tower-house tradition and Stirling Tolbooth has a shapely lead-covered steeple. The latter is by Bruce to whom Prestonfield is also attributed.

dinburgh, Prestonfield House 1687 by W. Bruce. Exterior and Drawing Room Chimneypiece

opetoun House, West Lothian, West Front 1702

Drumlanrig Castle, Dumfriesshire, 1679–90 by J. Smith. View of Garden Fronts and Detail of North Entrance Porch

James Smith, a son-in-law of Robert Mylne, who had worked on Holyroodhouse and who was appointed Overseer of the Royal Works in 1683, may yet prove to be a key figure in the Palladian movement. He designed the quite unique Canongate Kirk at Edinburgh, and at Drumlanrig seems to have been responsible for an equally unusual mansion. Based on an early seventeenth-century design, possibly by Wallace, it was completed in 1690 as a courtyard composition with clear allusions to Heriot's and Holyroodhouse and the works of Wallace, Mylne and Bruce, a fascinating mixture of Netherlandish Mannerism and Baroque. His tall Melville House (1697-1701) with detached wings and garden pavilions derives from Bruce's work and that of Roger Pratt in England. At Dalkeith, he incorporated an earlier dwelling in a symmetrical mansion with a pediment and a giant order of Corinthian pilasters.

Smith was partnered by Alexander McGill, architect of Newbattle and New Greyfriars churches, on the early part of Yester House to be succeeded by William Adam, whose works more properly belong to the Georgian period.

Melville House, Fife, 1697–1701 by J. Smith

Dalkeith House, Midlothian c.1705 by J. Smith

The larger burghs were laid out in medieval times around a great church or a monastery, a royal or a feudal castle, a river or a road crossing, a harbour or a combination of these. Though few medieval buildings survived, the town plans remained unaltered until the era of industrial expansion. The east coast ports developed greatly during the sixteenth and seventeenth centuries and the eighteenth saw the creation of formally planned towns and villages.

Stirling Bridge, 15th Century. Two of its four arches

St. Andrews, Fife, West Port 1589

# Scots Burghs

## 16th to 18th CENTURY

Above: Preston, East Lothian, Cross early
17th Century
Above right: Crail, Fife, Tolbooth 16th Century
and c.1800
Right: Culross, Fife, Tolbooth 1626, Tower 1783
Below: Culross, Fife, Market Cross and The Study

The characteristic town layout was normally dominated by the High Street (or Gait), off which lesser wynds and vennels branched, with the market place either as a widened portion of the street or a separate space. Pends under the houses led to the gardens or closes behind, which later tended to be built over, and the garden 'head dykes' formed a continuous perimeter wall around the burgh. While towns like Edinburgh and Stirling had formal defensive walls, portions of which survive, the 'back dykes' were intended primarily to ensure the entrance and exit of traffic through the town gates or 'ports', at which duties were levied. The most complete surviving town gateway is the West Port of St. Andrews. Riverside towns like Aberdeen, Ayr, Dumfries and Stirling have fine medieval bridges.

After the church, the Tolbooth or Town House, was the principal edifice. It comprised council chamber, court room and prison and was at first a tower structure, as at Tain, and later a hall and attached tower, approached generally by a forestair. Nearby, the town cross, usually a pillar with a heraldic finial, stood upon a stepped base or an elevated platform from which proclamations were made. Other public buildings were the merchant and trade guild halls, educational establishments like the College of Glasgow or Heriot's Hospital, Edinburgh (63), and charitable institutions like Cowane's Hospital, Stirling (63), and Dunbar's Hospital, Inverness.

Edinburgh, Knox's House
16th Century

2. Crail, Fife, Harbour
3. Linlithgow, St. Michael's Well 1720

Earlier houses of timber and thatch were replaced by sixteenth- and seventeenth-century stone dwellings with harled walls and slated or pantiled roofs and sometimes quaint timber galleries and superstructures. The houses which formed a complete and continuous façade often presented crowstepped and shaped gables to the street, and in some cases a ground-level street arcade with shopping and business space. The larger houses of nobles and lairds took the form of tower-houses like MacLellan's Castle, Kirkcudbright or Fordell Lodging, Inverkeithing or formal courtyard mansions like Argyll Lodging at Stirling, the Palace of Culross and Tankerness House, Kirkwall.

1. Gifford, East Lothian
2. Stirling, Argyll Lodging 1630–74
3. Pittenweem, Fife
Below: Edinburgh, West Bow Houses ,
 17th and early 18th Centuries

Airds House, Argyll, 1738

Edinburgh University, Centre 1789–94
by R. Adam, Curved Colonnades
1815–28 by W. H. Playfair, Dome
1887 by R. R. Anderson

Edinburgh, Royal High School 1829
by T. Hamilton

William Adam, senior, succeeded James Smith as Scotland's leading architect. The robust individuality of his style, a compound of Vanbrugh-Gibbs Baroque, Palladian and Scots native traditions, is evident in works like Hopetoun and Duff House (16), and in the *Vitruvius Scoticus* drawings.

An ascendant Palladianism is illustrated in Scottish houses like Paxton (*c.*1760), Sir William Chambers' Duddingston (1768), in smaller mansions like Airds (1738) and Glendoick (*c.*1760) and to some extent in early Robert and John Adam creations like Dumfries House and the Hopetoun pavilions. Later, Robert Adam and his brothers infused the exhausted Palladian theme with a new lightsomeness seen in houses like Newliston, street architecture like Charlotte Square (77), public buildings like Glasgow Trades House or Edinburgh Register House and University and the elegant interiors of Culzean and Mellerstain. Versatile Robert Mylne, architect and civil engineer, designed Galloway House, Cally House and most that is best in Inveraray, while John Baxter did comparable work at Fochabers and the Merchants' Hall, Edinburgh.

Advanced neo-Classical buildings were designed by the Elliot brothers, Robert Reid, William Burn and Gillespie Graham of Edinburgh and William Stark of Glasgow. Fully fledged Greek Revival work was done in a masterly way by W. H. Playfair and Thomas Hamilton in Edinburgh, David Hamilton in Glasgow and Archibald Simpson and John Smith in Aberdeen.

petoun House, West Lothian, East Front
.1721-60 by W., J. and R. Adam

Yester House, East Lothian, Saloon c.1760

ellerstain House, Berwickshire, Library
778 by R. Adam

Georgian Classical details made their appearance within the vernacular context of older burghs like Haddington or St. Andrews, as did public buildings and houses of more academic design. Expansions took place in regularly planned street schemes in many towns, the most spectacular being the New Town of Edinburgh, where, after some smaller schemes, James Craig's plan of 1767 initiated a series of large scale developments which continued into Victorian times. Until Robert Adam's Charlotte Square design (1791) no unified street elevations were attempted but this became fairly general practice thereafter.

Associated with agricultural developments, numerous planned towns and villages were laid out by improving lairds as a setting for local trades and industry. Some new settlements like Deanston, New Lanark and Stanley were associated with factories, mills or foundries, while fishing ports like Tobermory and Ullapool were founded by the British Fisheries Society and others by private landowners. Small towns like Fochabers, Inveraray and Ormiston represent the translation of older communities to new sites, while Inveresk, Midlothian is a unique suburban development with houses of late seventeenth- and eighteenth-century date.

The smaller town plans are generally of rectangular grid form with one or more squares and public buildings at focal points. Eaglesham (1769), however, was an unusual triangular plan around a central green and mill. Houses are commonly two or three storey vernacular structures with Classical embellishments.

Eaglesham, Renfrewshire, 18th Century

Inveraray, Argyll, c.1780 R. Mylne. Church 1802

Edinburgh, 35 St. Andrew Square 1769

w Town of Edinburgh

rlotte Square, c.1800

Charlotte Square, North Side 1791 by R. Adam

The cult of the picturesque produced landscaped parks with architectural incidents like gazebos, grottoes and mock ruins. The literary Romantic movement likewise provoked a revival of Gothic castellated and ecclesiastical architecture which had little reference to authentic medieval building. At first planning adhered to current Classical precepts. Moreover, until the mid-nineteenth century any allusions to historic styles were to exotic English ones.

Culzean Castle, Ayrshire, 1771-' by R. Adam

Inveraray Castle (1745-61) (16), designed by Roger Morris and based on a Vanbrugh sketch plan, has classical interiors by Robert Mylne. To the same phase belong Melville Castle (1786), Stobo (1805-11) and Taymouth (1806-10). Taymouth, like Stobo, by the Elliot brothers, with later additions, is outstanding. Robert Adam's Mellerstain (1770), based on his Ugbrooke in Devon, was followed by his castles of Culzean, Oxenfoorde, Seton and Pitfour. To this school belong John Paterson's Eglinton and the Elliots' Loudon. Duns and Duninald by Gillespie Graham are notable asymmetrical compositions.

Ecclesiastical Gothic was employed by Gillespie Graham at Cambusnethan and by Burn at Blairquhan and Carstairs while Abbotsford, Sir Walter Scott's home, is the harbinger of Victorian Scots Baronial.

Typical early Gothic Revival churches are Farnell, Kilmorich, Portsoy Catholic chapel and St. John's Episcopal church, Edinburgh.

2. Melville Castle, Midlothian, 1786 by J. Playfair
3. Abbotsford House, Roxburghshire, 1816-23 by E. Blore and W. Atkinson

Taymouth
Castle,
Perthshire,
Staircase
Hall 1806-10
by A. and J.
Elliot

Kilmorich
Church,
Argyll,
1816

Edinburgh,
St. John's
Episcopal
Church
1818 by
W. Burn

Portsoy
Catholic
Chapel,
Banffshire,
1829

Aberfeldy Bridge, Perthshire, 1733 by W. Adam

Kelso Bridge, Roxburghshire, 18 by J. Rennie

Craigellachie Bridge, Banffshire, 1815 by T. Telford

Avon Aqueduct, Stirlingshire, 1822 by H. Baird

The military 'pacification' following the Jacobite risings was marked by improvements at the castles of Dumbarton, Edinburgh and Stirling and in the Highlands by new barracks and forts and a network of military roads. The most notable architectural feature of the last is William Adam's Aberfeldy Bridge (1733).

Towards the end of the eighteenth century, the development of roads, bridges and harbours fell to distinguished civil engineers like John Smeaton, John Rennie and Thomas Telford. Smeaton's best bridges are at Perth and Banff, Rennie's at Kelso and Telford's at Dunkeld, Dean (Edinburgh) and Craigellachie, the last an 1815 essay in cast iron. At Hutton, Samuel Brown erected the first British suspension bridge in 1820, while of the many canal acqueducts that of Hugh Baird over the Avon is probably the most impressive.

nnockburn, Stirlingshire, Royal
George Mill c.1825

Edinburgh, Dean Village, Detail of Flour Mill
1806

Expanding industries produced new types of buildings. Some, like the foundries of Bonawe or Furnace, are austere functional structures of traditional masonry construction. The Wilsontown furnaces, now fragmentary, had a Roman monumentality while that at Muirkirk was given a robust Gothic treatment to form a focal feature from the manager's house in the village. At Perth, Dr. Anderson's waterworks (1832) were designed as an imposing Classical composition. Improved textile machinery was housed in numerous large mills, some with associated model villages like New Lanark, Stanley or Catrine. Corn mills vary from small traditional rural structures to the monumental buildings erected in the cities.

Perth, Waterworks 1832 by A. Anderson

Historicism expressed in both Classical and Romantic idioms is the salient feature of Victorian architecture. A Greek Revival carry-over is well illustrated by Playfair's Royal College of Physicians (1845) (17) and later by the genius of Alexander ('Greek') Thomson of Glasgow in Caledonia Road and St. Vincent churches and his terraces and houses. A popular Italian Renaissance revival marked commercial and public buildings like Charles Wilson's Royal Faculty of Procurators (1854) and J. T. Rochead's Bank of Scotland, St. Vincent's Place (1869) in Glasgow. Edinburgh examples are Robert Matheson's General Post Office (1866), David Bryce's Baroque Bank of Scotland (1870) and Rowand Anderson's Medical School (1888) and McEwan Hall (1890) towards the close of the century.

Moray Place, Strathbungo, 1859 by A. Thomson

Right: 336–56 Sauchiehall Street c. 1865
 by A. Thomson
Below right: Caledonia Road Church 1867
 by A. Thomson
Below: Custom House, 1840 by G. L. Taylor

Under the Romantic aegis, Gothic, more antiquarian than hitherto, all but monopolized church design. Quite outstanding is Edinburgh's Tolbooth Church (1844) by Gillespie Graham and Pugin, but the churches of F. T. Pilkington, contemporary and Gothic counterpart of 'Greek' Thomson, in a Teutonic idiom are the most imaginative of the period. In later churches, something of Scottish tradition made a tardy appearance in features like crown steeples and the Hiberno-Romanesque style later adopted by MacGregor Chalmers. Notable landmarks in this revival of native tradition are Kemp's Scott Monument (1844) designed as a church crossing and open spire, with details drawn from Melrose and J. T. Rochead's Wallace Monument (1869), a rugged tower with buttressed crown top.

Gothic was deemed equally appropriate for public buildings like Glasgow's Stock Exchange (1857), Dundee's Albert Institute (1874) and the National Portrait Gallery (1890), while a Franco-Scottish Baronial style was employed for municipal buildings at Aberdeen (1880), Annan (1877), Dunfermline (1879) and elsewhere. Certain collegiate associations doubtless accounted for Gothic educational buildings like New College, Edinburgh (1846), Glasgow University (1870), and Fettes College, Edinburgh (1870) the last in a French *château* manner.

Dunrobin Castle, Sutherland, 1845–51 by C. Barry

Kelso, Roxburghshire, Church of St. John's – Edenside 1867 by F. T. Pilkington

Stirling,
Wallace
Monument
1869
by J. T.
Rochead

Edinburgh,
Bank of
Scotland
1870 by
D. Bryce

Glasgow,
Stock
Exchange
1877 by
J. Burnet

Dunfermline,
Town House
1879
by J. C.
Walker

Edinburgh, Donaldson's Hospital 1854 by
W. H Playfair

Glasgow, Grosvenor Terrace
1855 by J. T. Rochead

The Scots Baronial vogue initiated by Abbotsford received royal approbation in Balmoral (1853-56) (17), the joint creation of William Smith and the Prince Consort. Numerous paper-conceived castles followed. More exotic styles were also used like Playfair's Tudor-Jacobean at Floors (1838) and Donaldson's Hospital (1854) or the Italianate Gothic of Rowand Anderson at Mount Stuart (c.1895).

Urban expansions on earlier Georgian lines continued, now marked by Italian Renaissance details, bay windows and plate glass and later by Scots Baronial and other features. Suburban terraces of single or double-storey houses, sometimes with Grecian details, made their appearance with the detached villa as an urban innovation. Later in the century model workers' dwellings, in terrace form or flats, were built. Outstanding among these is Well Court, Edinburgh (1884), built as a neighbourhood unit with a community hall.

Edinburgh, Eglinton Crescent
1875 by J. Chesser

Edinburgh, Well Court 1884 by S. Mitchell

Glasgow, Gardiner's Stores 1856 by J. Baird

Edinburgh, Royal Scottish Museum 1861 by Captain Fowke

Paisley, Anchor Mills 1871-83

Against the prevalent historicism serious essays were made to come to terms with novel building techniques in new kinds of structure like covered markets, museums and industrial buildings. Masonry traditions and structural skill produced fine road and railway bridges, workshops like Elder's Engine Works, Glasgow (c. 1860), or the Anchor Mills, Paisley and numerous factories and distilleries. Wrought and cast iron were used to span railway stations like St. Enoch's and Queen Street, Glasgow, and were effectively allied with traditional architectural forms in buildings like Gardiner's Stores, Glasgow (1856), the Royal Botanic Garden palm house (1858) and the Royal Scottish Museum (1861). The summit of cast iron construction is seen in Edinburgh's North Bridge (1897) while the cantilevered Forth Railway Bridge (1890) represented the development of steel as a building material.

At the turn of the century, the Art Nouveau work of Charles Rennie Mackıntosh earned international fame but had little impact in Scotland. Most architects adhered to interpretations of historical styles, principally Gothic for churches, a florid Classicism or Netherlandish Mannerism for commercial and public buildings and various others for comfortable country houses.

In contrast to his advanced St. Peter's Church, Edinburgh (1908), Sir Robert Lorimer's houses, Thistle Chapel (1910) and National War Memorial (1927) represent the summit of the Romantic movement. Commercial premises by Sir John Burnet, in a deft masonry treatment of steel-framed structures, remotely echo Louis Sullivan's more notable Chicago buildings. Tait's St. Andrew's House, Edinburgh (1938), is typical of the Classical-based school with certain Dudok (Dutch) undertones. Extensive and mainly unimpressive housing developments on vaguely 'garden city' lines during inter-war years, established the general use of brick as a standard building material in contrast with native masonry traditions.

lasgow, School of Art 1897–1909
y C. R. Mackintosh

dinburgh, Forsyth's Stores 1907
by J. J. Burnet, enlarged 1925

Edinburgh, St. Andrew's House 1938 by T. S. Tait

The end of the Second World War saw the general acceptance of modern architecture as an idiom appropriate to the hospitals and schools, airports, public utilities and industries of the welfare state. In urban areas 'garden city' notions linger, but new ideas are manifested in high flats and office buildings and in developments like the new towns of East Kilbride, Glenrothes and Cumbernauld with their shopping centres and pedestrian precincts. Public buildings tend to conform with the current outlook and churches, with varying degrees of success, seek in modern design to satisfy theological and liturgical needs.

Edinburgh Castle, The Scottish National War Memorial 1927 by R. S. Lorimer

Forth Road Bridge 1958–64 by Mott, Hay and Anderson; beyond, the Railway Bridge 1890 by J. Fowler and B. Baker

Edinburgh
University,
David Hume
Tower 1963
by Matthew
and Johnson
- Marshall

East Kilbride,
Lanarkshire,
St. Bride's
Church 1963
by J.A.Coia

Edinburgh,
Royal Botanic
Gardens, Plant
House 1967 by
G.A.H.Pearce

# Vernacular Architecture

North Uist Cottage

Auchtermuchty Cottage

Crovie, Banffshire

The charming vernacular architecture of Scotland, which varies from district to district, is the product of local conditions, traditions, materials and craftsmanship. It has been influenced by and in turn has affected more sophisticated ways of building.

Scotland's abundance of building stones resulted in a lengthy tradition of masonry construction including dry and clay built rubble and external lime-based harling. Roofing materials like heather, straw or reed thatch, flagstones, slates and pantiles were also formative factors in design. Native timber was much used in medieval building and in the cruck construction of certain types of Highland dwellings but few of these have survived.

Traditional Highland thatched houses, with regional variations, demonstrate by their contours their suitability for an open windswept terrain. In north Fife, the reeds of Lindores Loch provided an adequate roof covering for cottages of more formal design. Many north-east fishing villages and ports are so planned that their rows of slated or pantiled houses present sturdy gables towards the sea, as at Crovie.

The architectural idiom of lairds' houses and farms, with harled walls and slated roofs was employed also in parish churches in areas like Caithness. Georgian details of Classical or Gothic type were likewise incorporated in rural churches and other public buildings.

eswick House, Caithness

Dunnet Church, Caithness
Innerpeffry Library, Perthshire,
c.1750

verarity Church, Angus, 1754

Above: Auldgirth Inn, Dumfriesshi

Left: Tanhouse Brae, Culross, Fife

Tynet R.C. Church, Moray

Haddington, East Lothian

Small sixteenth- and seventeenth-century town houses used crowsteps, moulded doorways and dormers drawn from the vocabulary of more formal buildings. Similarly, motifs of Georgian Classical or Gothic form were effectively incorporated in small vernacular houses, inns and shops. Focus and unity is often given to the urban scene by the steeple or *flêche* of the tolbooth, not uncommonly a derivative of Baltic or Low Country vernacular.

A characteristic feature of the rural scene is the functional dovecot, which was in effect a larder of winter meat, controlled by Scots legislation. The earlier sixteenth-century bee-hive type was followed by others of lean-to, or, less commonly, gabled form. Later, more formal circular, square or polygonal designs were adopted.

Rural mills, like Preston, combine industrial functionalism with vernacular building traditons, and farm steadings vary between informal courtyard groupings and modestly stylized symmetrical compositions.

Preston Mill,
East Lothian

Dirleton,
East Lothian,
Castle
Dovecot

Pencait-
land,
Dovecot

The distribution of Scotland's best architecture corresponds in the main with the more populous areas of the country, the south, central and north-east, with other examples of varying interest thinly scattered over the more scenically spectacular north and west. Inclusion of a building in a tour does not imply public access. The following tours are planned to cover as far as possible representative examples of all architectural types and periods. They lend themselves to endless permutations according to personal inclinations and interests.

ABBREVIATIONS    Ab = Abbey, Cas = Castle, Cath = Cathedral, Ch = Church, Ho = House, Vill = Village

## TOUR ONE :- SOUTH EAST

Emphasis: Churches and Monasteries, Country Houses, Urban Architecture, Castles
EDINBURGH - MUSSELBURGH (Bridge, Town Ho, Inveresk Vill, Pinkie Ho) PRESTONPANS (Tower, Northfield, Hamilton Ho, Cross) SETON (Ch 15-16c) HADDINGTON (Ch 15c, Bridge, Town Hall and houses) - detour to LENNOXLOVE (Ho 15-17c) GIFFORD (Yester Ho 18c, Vill and Ch 18c) - DIRLETON (Cas 13c, Ch 17c) NORTH BERWICK (Town Ho, Harbour, Tantallon Cas 14-16c) DUNGLASS (Ch 15c) COLDINGHAM (Priory 12-13c) PAXTON (Ho 18c) LADYKIRK (Ch c.1500) COLDSTREAM (Bridge by Rennie) KELSO (Ab, Ch, Ednam Ho, Bridge by Rennie, Floors Cas 18-19c) NISBET (Ho 17-18c) JEDBURGH (Ab, Bridge, Queen Mary's Ho, Town ho) DRYBURGH (Ab) - detour to SMAILHOLM (Tower 16c) MELLERSTAIN (Ho by W & R Adam) - MELROSE (Ab, Cross, Darnick Tower 16c) ABBOTSFORD (Ho 19c) INNER-LEITHEN (Traquair Ho 16-18c) PEEBLES (Town Ho, Bridge, Neidpath Cas 14-17c) LYNE (Ch 17c) DROCHIL (Cas 16c) BIGGAR (Ch 1545) PENICUIK (Ho 18c, Ch 18c) ROSLIN (Cas 13-17c, Ch 15c) DALKEITH (Ho by J.Smith, Ch 15c, Bridge, Newbattle Ab & Ho) EDINBURGH.


## TOUR TWO :- FIFE & CENTRAL

Emphasis: Churches and Monasteries, Castles, Urban Architecture, Country houses
EDINBURGH - SOUTH QUEENSFERRY (Carmelite Ch, Tolbooth, Dalmeny Ch, Forth Bridges) - detour to DUNFERMLINE (Ab & Pal) CULROSS (Ab, Pal, Tolbooth & Ho's) - INVERKEITHING (Cross, Tolbooth, Fordell Lodging, Ho's) ABERDOUR (Cas 13-17c, Ch 12c and Aberdour Ho, 17-18c) INCHCOLM (Ab 12-15c) BURNTISLAND (Ch 16c, Somerville Ho 17c) KIRKCALDY (Ravens-craig Cas 15c, Dysart Ch 15c and Tolbooth 17c) ELIE ('Cas' 17c, Ch 17-19c) ST. MONANCE (Ch, Harbour and Ho's) PITTENWEEM (Priory, Ch, Cross, Kellie Lodging 17c, Harbour) ANSTRUTHER (E & W Ch's, E. Manse, Harbour, Ho's) - detour to KILRENNY (Ch Tower 15c) KELLIE (Cas 16c) - CRAIL (Ch, Tolbooth, Harbour, Ho's) ST. ANDREWS (Cath, Cas, Colleges, Ch, W Port, Harbour, Ho's) LEUCHARS (Ch 12c) DAIRSIE (Cas & Bridge 16c, Ch 17c) CUPAR (Ch 15-18c, Cross, Pub Bdgs & Ho's, Scotstarvit Tower 16c) MELVILLE (Ho by J Smith) FALKLAND (Pal, Town Ho & Ho's) KINROSS (Ho by W Bruce, Lochleven Cas 14c) TULLIBOLE (Cas 17c) ALDIE (Cas 16c) DOLLAR (Castle Campbell 15-16c, Academy and Town Ho's 19c) DUNBLANE (Cath 12-13c)

DOUNE (Cas 14c) STIRLING (Cas, Ch, Tolbooth, Ho's, Cambuskenneth Ab) AIRTH (Cas 16-19c, Dunmore Park 19c, 'Pineapple' 18c) LINLITHGOW (Pal, Ch, Town Ho) BLACKNESS (Cas 16-17c) BINNS (Ho 17 & 19c) HOPETOUN (Ho by W Bruce and W, R & J Adam) EDINBURGH

## TOUR THREE :- GLASGOW & SOUTH WEST

Emphasis: Castles, Churches & Monasteries, Urban Architecture

GLASGOW - PAISLEY (Ab 15c) KILMAURS (Tolbooth 18c, Rowallan Cas 16-17c) DUNDONALD (Cas 13-15c) SYMINGTON (Ch 12c) TARBOLTON (Ch 18c, Montgomerie Ho 19c) AYR (Bridges, Ch, Town Hall, Ho's) MAYBOLE (Cas 17c, Crossraguel Ab 15c) CULZEAN (Cas by R Adam) KILLOCHAN (Cas 16c) STRANRAER (Cas 16c, Town Hall 18c) KIRKMADRINE (Cross Slabs 5-6c) GLENLUCE (Ab 12-15c, Cas of Park 16c) MOCHRUM (Place 15-16c, Druchtag Motehill) WHITHORN (Priory, Mus, Town Hall) GALLOWAY HO (18c) KIRK-INNER (Cross 11c) NEWTON STEWART (Tolbooth 18c, Bridge by Rennie) GATE-HOUSE OF FLEET (Cardoness Cas 15c, Cally Ho by R Mylne) KIRKCUDBRIGHT (Cas 16c, Tolbooth 16c, Georgian Ho's) DUNDRENNAN (Ab 12-15c) ORCHARDTON TOWER (15c) CASTLE DOUGLAS (Threave Cas 14c) NEW ABBEY (Ab 13-15c) DUMFRIES (Bridge, Coll Ch, Mid Steeple, Caerlaverock Cas 13-17c, Comlongan Tower 15c, Ruthwell Cross 7-8c) AMISFIELD TOWER (1600) THORNHILL (Morton Cas 14c, Drumlanrig Cas 17c, Durisdeer Ch 17c) LANARK (Ch 18c, New Lanark 18 & 19c) CRAIGNETHAN CAS (15c) HAMIL-TON (Ch by W Adam, Mausoleum) BOTHWELL (Ch 15c, Cas 13-15c) GLASGOW.

## TOUR FOUR :- NORTH EAST

Emphasis: Churches & Monasteries, Castles, Urban Architecture, Country Houses.

PERTH (Ch, Bridge by Smeaton, Pub Bdgs & Ho's) KINFAUNS (Cas by R Smirke) PITFOUR (Cas by R Adam) DUNDEE (Ch Tower, Custom Ho, Camperdown Ho, Albert Inst, Claypotts Cas 16c) BROUGHTY FERRY (Cas 16c) ARBROATH (Ab 13-15c, Harbour, Mills) ST. VIGEANS (Ch 15c, Mus of Cross Slabs) MONTROSE (Ch 18-19c, Town Ho 18c, Academy 19c, Mills, Dun Ho 18c) - detour to ALLARDYCE (Cas 17c) ARBUTHNOTT (Ch 15c, Ho 18c) STONEHAVEN (Dunnottar Cas 15-17c, Tolbooth, Harbour) MUCHALLS (Cas 17c) ABERDEEN (Cath, King's Coll, Bridges, Pub Bdgs & Ho's) DRUM (Cas 13-17c) CRATHES (Cas 16c) MIDMAR (Cas 16-17c) CRAIGIEVAR (Cas 17c) HUNTLY (Cas 15-17c) BANFF (Duff Ho by W Adam, Cross, Bridge & Town Ho's) PORTSOY (Harbour & Town Ho's) CULLEN (Ch 15c, Cullen Ho 17c, Town Ho, Harbour) FOCHABERS Ch & Town 18c) ELGIN (Cath, Friary, Ch, Pub Bdgs & Ho's) PLUSCARDEN (Priory 13-15c) CRAIGELLACHIE (Bridge by Telford) DUFFTOWN (Ch 13 & 19c, Balvenie Cas 15-16c) AUCHINDOIR (Ch 13c) KILDRUMMY (Cas 13c, Ch 19c) ABOYNE (Cas 17c & later) EDZELL (Cas 16-17c) BRECHIN (Cath & Round Tower) RESTENNETH (Priory) GLAMIS (Cas 16-17c) MEIGLE (Mus of Carved Slabs) DUNKELD (Cath, Bridge by Telford & Ho's) PERTH.